decorating
with
papercraft

decorating with papercraft

25 Fresh and Eco-Friendly Projects for the Home

Clare Youngs

The Taunton Press

Dedicated to my four children, Milly, Florence, Henrietta, and Harvey, without whom this book may have been published years earlier, but would not have been so much fun to make!

The Taunton Press, Inc., 63 South Main Street, PO Box 5506, Newtown, CT 06470-5506
email: tp@taunton.com

First published in Great Britain in 2009 by Hamlyn, a division of Octopus Publishing Group Ltd
2–4 Heron Quays, London E14 4JP
www.octopusbooks.co.uk

ISBN: 978-1-60085-301-2

A CIP catalog record for this book is available from the Library of Congress.

Printed and bound in China

10 9 8 7 6 5 4 3 2 1

Disclaimer
The publisher cannot accept any legal responsibility or liability for accidents or damage arising from the use of any items mentioned in this book or in the carrying out of any of the projects.

contents

introduction

Paper, that most ordinary and extraordinary material, is something that we take for granted in our daily lives. We write on it, we read from it, we wrap our food in it, and we feed reams of it through our computer printers. But ever since the Chinese invented paper in 200 BC, people have looked beyond its use as a means of carrying information and have created beautifully decorated and useful craftworks by cutting, folding, and gluing.

Throughout the centuries, paper has enriched our lives. Think of the paper kites of Japan, the brightly colored tissue paper cutouts of Mexico, the paper silhouettes of southern Asia—this is a craft that has been used in festivals, celebrations, and ceremonies around the world. Craftspeople working today use skills that have been passed on from generation to generation, from the art of découpage seen in the elegant furniture of 18th-century Italy to the intricate paper-cuts of China. Designers are continually finding new ways to express their creativity through paper. Clothing, jewelry, furniture—the boundaries are expanding all the time.

In a world where we have to conserve our resources, it is important to be able to use recycled material and the projects in this book do just that. If you root through your recycling bin at the end of the week, you'll be able to salvage bits of cardstock that can be used as a base for some of the projects. Look more closely at food labels or even junk mail: there may be interesting areas of color or lettering you could utilize. At garage sales and secondhand stores, look out for old maps, books, and, in particular, old music scores, which often have wonderful typography on the covers. Keep scraps of wrapping paper, and tear out the unused pages from old notebooks to reinvent into something handmade and unique.

Modern interiors have moved on from the minimalist 1990s. Today, it's all about creating a space that says something about you as an individual. These projects will allow you to customize your home. The craft may be an ancient one, but with paper you can create stylish and contemporary pieces to update an interior, make a stunning focal point, or provide a thoughtful gift.

The projects are graded in skill level from 1 to 4 "scissors" and range from the very simple (for example, the Party Garland on page 14) to those that are more challenging (such as the Ornate Picture Frame on page 102). Whatever projects you attempt, they will encourage you to look at paper in a new light. As you develop your own ideas and style, your eyes will be opened to the endless possibilities of a material that is cheap and readily available to us all. Don't be afraid to adapt projects and experiment—you will be amazed at what you can achieve!

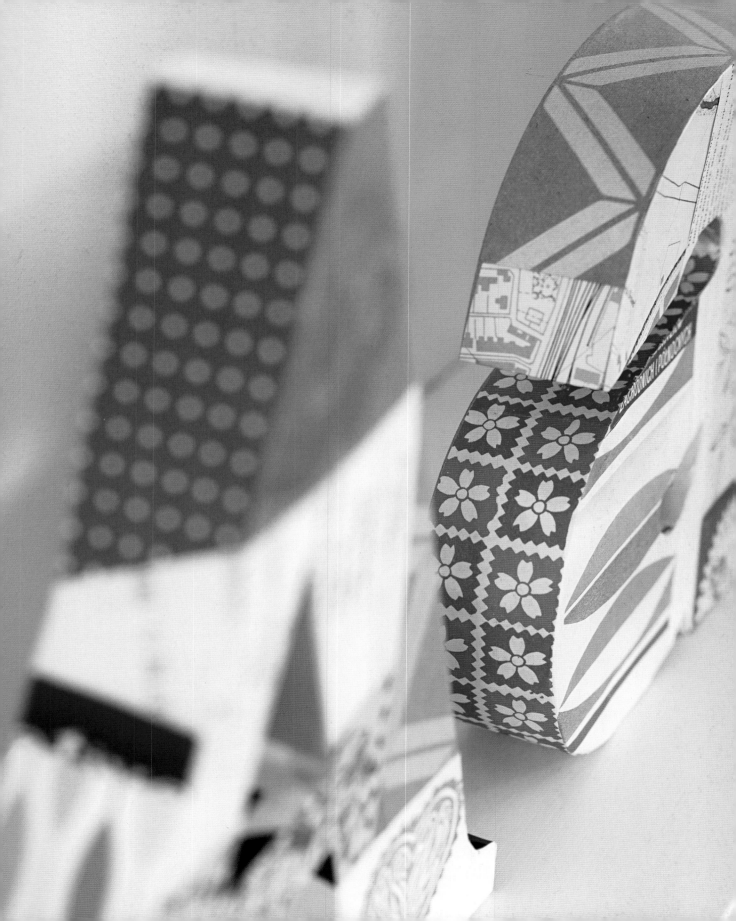

tools and materials

To make the projects in this book, you will need certain essential items of

equipment, available from craft and hardware stores or artists' suppliers.

A huge range of paper and cardstock of different types and weights can be found

at similar outlets. You can also be creative with recycled material.

Tools

Papercraft does not require you to buy a lot of expensive equipment. All the tools you will need to make the projects are listed in the sidebar on the opposite page. In addition, there are a few other tools that are useful but not essential. A bone folder is a spatula-type implement that you press along a fold to make it sharp. A soft brush is handy to use to sweep off erasings left after removing pencil marks. Ordinary clothes pins are also useful as clamps to keep glued items in place while they are drying.

Hole punches

For a number of the projects, you will need a hole punch. These come in a variety of types and you can buy them from craft stores. A hammer punch is a metal tube with interchangeable heads. To punch a hole, you position the head and tap the base of the tube with a hammer. This type of punch enables you to place holes very precisely, which is useful when making a pattern of holes, for example for the White Cardstock Candle Shades (see page 114).

There is also a rotary type of punch, which has punch heads on a wheel. You position the head, then squeeze the arms of the punch together (as you would a pair of pliers) to punch out the hole. Both the hammer and the rotary type of punch are quite cheap, but you can also buy more elaborate punches with many interchangeable heads, which allow you to press down with the palm of your hand to cut the hole. These tend to be expensive, but do have multiple uses.

A hammer punch with interchangeable heads in three different sizes (such as $1/16$ in., $1/8$ in., and $1/4$ in.) will work well for the full range of projects featured in this book.

Adhesives

The projects require various types of glue. Some use two different glues plus an adhesive tape. This is the range of adhesives used in the projects:

- **Glue stick made of clear glue.** This goes on smoothly and never seems to clog up.

- **White school glue.** Drying to become clear and flexible, this white glue is very useful.

- **Strong, quick-drying, clear glue.** A tube of this is essential. It is often necessary for the glue to dry quickly, before you can move on to the next step of the project.

- **Spray glue (or spray-mount glue).** This is used in some projects. Follow the manufacturer's instructions for use carefully and always wear a mask. If possible, use spray glue outside. If you have to use it inside, lay down lots of newspaper and make sure you have proper ventilation.

- **Adhesive tape.** Double-sided tape and masking tape are both used frequently; cellophane tape occasionally.

Materials

The projects in this book use different weights of paper and cardstock. Paper and cardstock is measured in gsm (grams per square meter), and the higher the gsm, the thicker the paper. For a project that requires a thick paper, such as cartridge paper, look for a weight of about 120 gsm. For thin cardstock, choose a weight of about 160 gsm. For thick cardstock, choose a weight of about 200+ gsm.

The range of paper types is vast. Paper manufacturers all over the world are continually coming up with exciting new varieties, which are readily available to buy. Choose from the textural, handmade papers of India, China, Mexico, and Egypt or the elegantly decorated, marbled and patterned paper of Italy and France. Japanese washi papers come in an array of rich colors and the chiyogami papers are exquisitely patterned. You can buy paper that is flocked, embellished with real flower petals, translucent, embroidered, or metallic.

As you explore the possibilities of papercraft, you can experiment with using different types of bought and recycled paper to complement and enhance your designs and make something really unique. Once you get hooked on papercraft, the opportunities to create exciting pieces are endless.

Essential tools

Scissors (1 large pair and 1 small pair for fine cutting)

Craft knife

Cutting mat

Hole punch that can punch three sizes of holes

Hammer (if using hammer punch)

Ruler

Set square

Table knife for scoring

Pencils: No. 3 (hard) and No. 2 (softer)

Sharpener

Eraser

Stapler

papercraft techniques

One of the joys of papercraft is that it does not require the use of complicated techniques. However, you will need to use templates (sometimes enlarging them to the desired size) and to cut, score, and fold accurately. A few tips are given below.

Enlarging templates

Some of the templates printed on pages 118–126 need to be enlarged using a photocopier. If that is the case, the required percentage enlargement is given. If you don't have access to a photocopier, you can enlarge templates by hand. First, trace the template onto graph paper using the tracing technique described below. Then, on a larger, blank piece of paper, draw up a grid that contains the same number of squares but has been enlarged by the appropriate percentage. You can then scale up the template by hand, copying the lines in each square of the graph paper into the corresponding square of the enlarged grid.

For the larger size of Airplane Mobile (see page 72), the templates need to be enlarged in segments, as does the template for the Monochrome Photo Cubes (see page 76). Instructions are given in the projects for how to do this.

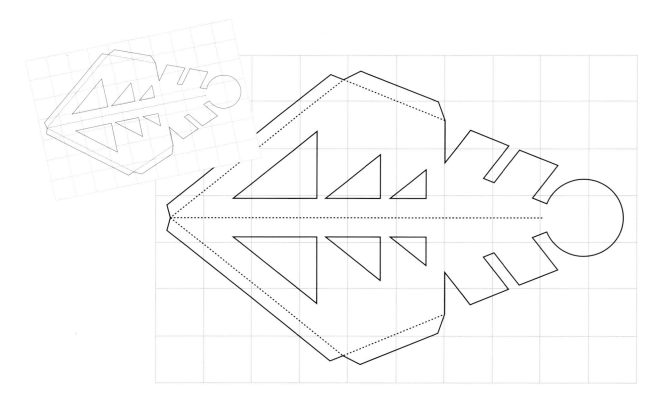

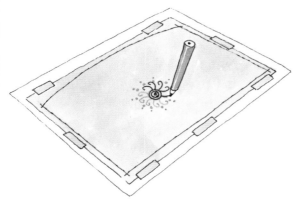

Tracing

Many of the projects require you to transfer a template (see pages 118–126) onto your chosen cardstock or paper. To do this, fix tracing paper over the template with masking tape. Trace the lines with a hard (No. 3) pencil. Release the tracing paper, turn it over and, using a softer (No. 2) pencil, go over the lines. Now turn the tracing paper over again, and secure in position on the cardstock or paper with masking tape. Go over the lines once more with a hard pencil (using a hard pencil at this point gives an accurate line). Remove the tracing paper. You will now be able to see the lines of the template on the cardstock.

When a template is large, with lots of corners and straight lines, it is easier to prick through the tracing paper with a pin at all the meeting corners, then remove the tracing paper and join up the pin marks using a sharp pencil and ruler.

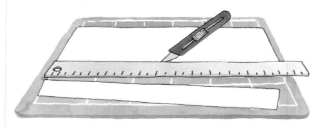

Cutting

When using scissors, always keep the paper moving, not the scissors, to give you more control.

Sometimes, it is easier to cut with a craft knife. Check that the blade is sharp and always put a cutting mat underneath the cardstock. When cutting straight lines, use a metal ruler and make sure the blade is in contact with the ruler at all times. Cut toward you, applying equal pressure along the length of the cut.

When cutting cardboard, it is often impossible to cut through it with one pass with the knife. Apply light pressure for the first cut, and then repeat until you have cut right through the thickness.

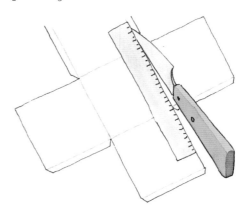

Scoring

Scoring is an important part of papercraft. Usually, it is best to draw a line with a sharpened hard pencil. Line up a metal ruler with the line, and using the blunt side of a table knife, score down the line, keeping the blade in contact with the ruler.

For the Corrugated Cardboard Letter Rack (see page 80), a different type of scoring is required. Here you apply gentle pressure with the sharp side of a craft knife to break the surface of the cardstock, without cutting through it.

Folding

Fold away from you, lining up the edges of the cardstock carefully. Press down to create a crease with the palm of your hand. For an extra-sharp line, use a bone folder to press along the fold. Sometimes it may be necessary to make an incision along the fold line, which breaks the surface of the cardstock (see Scoring, above).

flowers and frills

tools and materials

Tissue paper, 15 in. x 20 in. per tassel
Pencils (No. 3 and No. 2)
Ruler
Scissors
Craft knife
Cutting mat
Plain colored paper, 1 in. x 1$^1/_2$ in. per
   tassel binding
Strong, quick-drying glue
Template on page 118
Tracing paper
Masking tape
Patterned paper, 1$^1/_2$ in. x 7 in. per
   decorative strip
String measuring length of finished garland

This garland, fashioned from brightly colored tissues and scraps of contrasting paper, makes for a really festive atmosphere. It can be made to any length you desire. So, if you are having a party, hang it across the room; if you are having friends over for dinner, string it across a table.

party garland

1 To make the first tassel, fold the tissue paper in half lengthwise, then in half again and then in half again. Fold the piece in half widthwise.

2 Working toward the fold, cut six strips each about 3/8 in. wide. Cut along the outer edges too, to avoid double-width strips. Stop about 1 1/2 in. from the central fold.

3 Open out the piece again widthwise, then fold in half lengthwise and then in half again, so that you are left with a thin central strip with a cut fringe on either side.

4 Fold the piece in half to form a tassel. Cut out a binding strip measuring 1 in. x 1¹/₂ in. Bind the tassel piece by folding it along the central fold line and wrapping the binding around the tassel about ¹/₂ in. from the top. Secure with a dab of glue.

5 Fan out the ends of the tassel. Repeat the process to make as many tassels as desired.

6 Make the decorative strips. Trace the template on page 118 and transfer to the patterned paper (see page 11). Cut out as many as needed using scissors or a craft knife and cutting mat.

7 Put the garland together. Thread the tassels onto the string, alternating with the decorative strips. To attach the decorative strips, fold each strip over the string and glue the ends together.

tools and materials
Spray glue
Patterned paper, 3 in. x 8 in. per flower
Thin white cardstock, 3 in. x 8 in. per flower
Templates on page 119
Tracing paper
Masking tape
Pencils (No. 3 and No. 2)
Scissors
Craft knife
Ruler
Cutting mat
Lampshade

Find a lampshade you have grown tired of then customize it to create this individual and striking project. You can use up small pieces of wrapping paper and leftover scraps from other projects. The flowers are simple to make, and on another occasion you could make them to use as decorations for wrapped gifts.

flower
lampshade

1 Spray-glue the patterned paper for each flower to a piece of thin white cardstock.

2 Trace the three petal templates and the flower centerpiece template on page 119 and transfer them to the patterned paper (see page 11). Cut two of each petal and one centerpiece for each flower. Cut out the slots in the petals.

3 Take the centerpiece and cut a fringe where shown on the template. Fold the piece in half with the pattern facing inward.

6 Using the craft knife, make small slits all over the lampshade, about 2¼ in. apart, to hold the flowers. Slip the stem of each centerpiece through a slit. The thickness of the stem will hold it in position. Continue adding flowers until the shade is covered. When hanging the shade, use a bulb with a maximum of 60W.

4 Push the petals onto the centerpiece one at a time. Make sure that you do it in order: use a differently angled slot each time so that the petals spread out around the centerpiece.

5 Fan out the fringe on the centerpiece. Bend each petal up toward the centerpiece to form the flower shape.

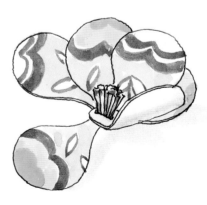

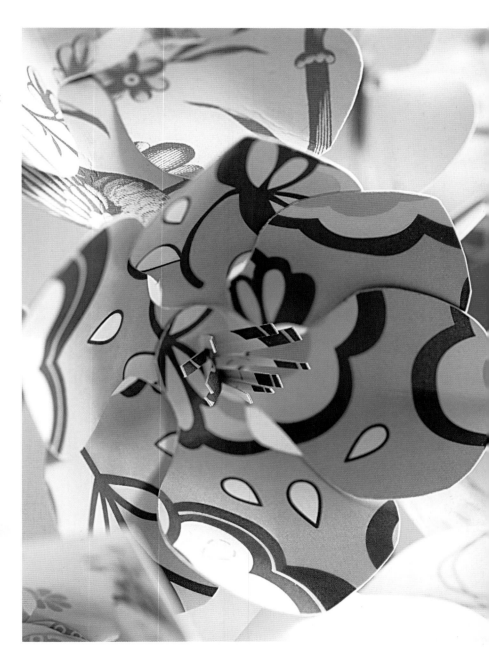

skill level

tools and materials
1 sheet white tissue paper, 30 in. x 20 in.
Pencils (No. 3 and No. 2)
Scissors
Ruler
Craft knife
Cutting mat
White cardstock, length as for fish's mouth x 1/2 in.
Glue stick
Double-sided tape
Templates on page 119
Tracing paper
Masking tape
Tissue paper in different colors
Thin gold paper
Hole punch
String

Ornamental wind socks have a long history in China and Japan, where they are considered a symbol of good luck. In Japan, they are called *koinobori* and are flown every year on Children's Day. The wind socks make original party decorations, especially during summer, when they look wonderful hanging from the branches of trees.

asian
flying fish

1 Fold the white tissue paper in half. Following the illustration, draw a fish shape freehand on the tissue paper. Cut out the shape.

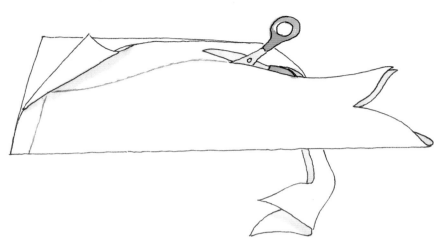

2 Open out the tissue paper. Measure the head end and cut a piece of cardstock to this length, making it $1/2$ in. wide. Using a glue stick, glue the cardstock along the tissue to form the inside of the fish's mouth.

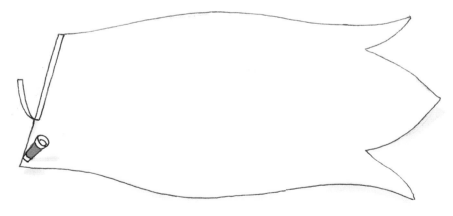

3 Curve the cardstock strip around into a circle, overlap the ends by a small amount and secure with double-sided tape.

4 Spread glue along one long side of the fish, tapering the glue to a point at the cardstock strip, and stick the two sides of the fish together.

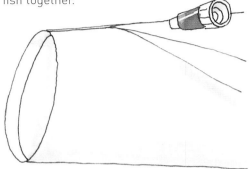

5 Trace the templates for the eye and scales (see page 119), transfer the outlines to the colored tissue paper and gold paper (see page 11) and cut them out.

6 Use a glue stick to attach the decorative shapes to both sides of the fish.

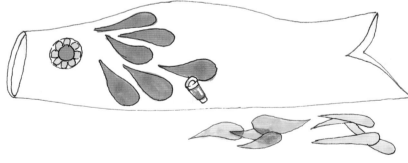

7 Punch a small hole on either side of the fish's mouth, through the cardstock. Attach string for hanging the fish.

skill level

tools and materials
Pencil (No. 2)
Ruler
Craft knife
Cutting mat
Tissue paper, 2 in. x 10 in. per
    tealight lantern
Translucent paper, $3^1/_2$ in. x 10 in. per
    tealight lantern
Thin gold paper, $^1/_2$ in. x 10 in. per
    tealight lantern
Sewing machine and pretty thread or glue stick
Double-sided tape
Glass tealight holders, about 3 in. tall x $2^3/_4$ in. diameter

For this project, pretty, translucent paper is used to make paper shades. These fit over a glass containing a tealight. Craft stores, especially those that sell paper for scrapbooking, will have a good selection of papers. When the tealight is lit, the simple paper shade transforms the candle into a glowing jewel-like decoration.

tealight **lanterns**

1 Cut a strip of tissue paper 2 in. x 10 in., a strip of translucent paper 3½ in. x 10 in., and a strip of thin gold paper ½ in. x 10 in.

2 Fold the tissue paper in half lengthwise and place it ½ in. from the top of the translucent paper. Put the gold paper on top, in the center of the tissue paper.

3 Sew through the layers of tissue, gold strip, and translucent paper. Alternatively, you can adhere the papers with glue. If you are making a few tealights, you could vary the width of the tissue paper and gold paper.

4 Attach double-sided tape to one of the shorter sides of the rectangle of translucent paper. Draw the other side around and stick the edges together to form a cylinder that will fit around the tealight holder.

tools and materials
Thick white cardstock, 35 in. x 25 in.
Pencil (No. 3)
Ruler
Craft knife
Cutting mat
Stapler and staples
9 sheets silver leaf, 5$\frac{1}{2}$ in. x 5$\frac{1}{2}$ in.
4 sheets thin white cardstock, letter size
Size or spray glue
Tracing paper
Hole punch
Freezer bag ties (we used white) or very thin wire
Scissors or pliers
Double-sided tape
String or strong thread

It is hard to believe that this waterfall decoration is made out of white cardstock and freezer bag ties. The silver leaf transforms the everyday materials into something very special and the decoration glimmers as the light catches it. Hang it near a window where it can sparkle in the sunlight.

silvery waterfall
decoration

1 Start by making the base for the decoration. Cut six strips of thick white cardstock: four measuring 7 in. long, one measuring 25 in. long, and one 16 1/2 in. long. Each strip should be 3/4 in. wide.

2 Bend the 16 1/2-in. strip into a small ring. Overlap the ends by about 1/2 in. and staple together. Repeat this with the 25-in. strip to form a larger ring.

3 Join the four 7-in. strips to the small ring. Place the ends of the strips at four equal intervals inside the ring and attach with a stapler.

4 Join the other end of the strips to the large ring. Again, place the ends of the strips at four equal intervals inside the ring and attach with a stapler.

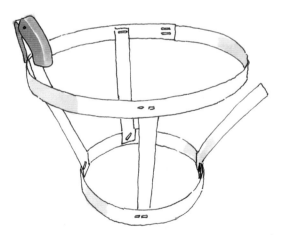

5 Now make the silvery panels. Arrange strips of silver leaf on the thin white cardstock. Place them randomly, filling the sheet but leaving gaps between each piece.

6 Now fix the silver leaf in place. Pick up a piece of silver leaf and brush size on the cardstock underneath. As it starts to dry and become tacky, apply the silver leaf and remove the backing paper. As an alternative, you can spray each piece of silver leaf lightly with glue, put in position and peel off the backing paper. Whichever method you use, rub the silver leaf through a sheet of tracing paper to smooth it down.

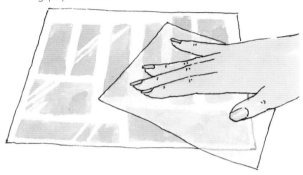

10 Work on the smaller rectangles in pairs. In each rectangle, punch a hole about 1/4 in. in from the center of one of the short sides. Join the rectangles together in groups of two, using freezer bag ties (cut in half as above) and leaving a gap of 1/8 in. between each one.

11 Attach double-sided tape to the top rectangle of each group of three rectangles. Attach to the large ring, leaving an 1/8-in. gap between each one.

7 Cut out 48 rectangles of silver-leafed cardstock measuring 2³/4 in. x 1¹/2 in. and 24 rectangles measuring 2³/4 in. x 1¹/4 in. Each rectangle should include randomly positioned amounts of silver leaf (see photograph on page 31).

8 Work on the larger rectangles in groups of three. In one rectangle, punch a small hole about 1/4 in. in from the center of both short sides. In the other two rectangles, punch a hole in one short side only.

9 Cut the freezer ties in half and use them to join the three rectangles, leaving a gap of 1/8 in. between each one.

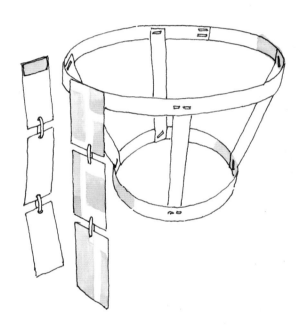

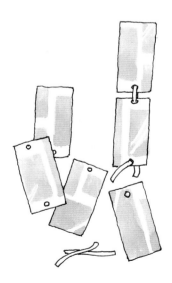

12 Attach the pairs of rectangles to the small ring in the same way.

13 Punch small holes for hanging at equal distances around the large ring. Thread a piece of string through each and knot on the inside. Tie the ends of the string together to hang up the decoration.

skill level

tools and materials

Spray glue

2 sheets patterned paper, about 5^1/$_2$ in. x 9 in. per bird

Thin cardstock, 5^1/$_2$ in. x 9 in. per bird (if patterned paper is very thin)

Templates on page 118

Tracing paper

Masking tape

Pencils (No. 3 and No. 2)

Scissors

Craft knife

Ruler

Cutting mat

Hole punch

Scorer

Double-sided tape

Needle

Thread for hanging

These gracious birds are made from scraps of eye-catching paper. You might like to make a few and hang them grouped together at different heights. A flock of birds would make an attractive decoration for a child's bedroom.

hanging **birds**

1 Using spray glue, stick two pieces of patterned paper together to form a double-sided rectangle. (If you are using thin paper, sandwich a piece of thin cardstock between the two sheets.)

2 Using the templates on page 118, trace the five pieces for each bird (one body, two large lower wings, and two small upper wings) and transfer to the double-sided rectangle of patterned paper (see page 11). Cut out the pieces.

3 Punch out the decorative holes where indicated on the template.

4 Score the flaps as indicated on the template and bend them into position.

5 Use double-sided tape to stick each upper wing over each lower wing.

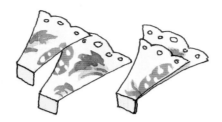

6 Use double-sided tape to attach a completed wing to each side of the bird's body.

7 Using a needle to pierce the cardstock, take a length of hanging thread through the bird's body just above the wings. Feed the ends of the thread through the bottom and top holes of the tail, before hanging up the bird.

tools and materials
Templates on page 120
Tracing paper
Masking tape
Pencils (No. 3 and No. 2)
Foam board, 8 in. x 10 in. x $^1/_4$ in.
Craft knife
Ruler
Cutting mat
Glue stick or spray glue
2 pieces patterned paper, 8 in. x 10 in.
Strong, quick-drying glue

This ring holder has been inspired by the stencils used in the Asian tradition of creating henna patterns on hands. An opulent paper completes the look. The back of the ring holder is also covered with paper, so that the two sides will look equally attractive if the holder is kept on a dressing table and reflected in a mirror.

ring holder

4 Repeat to cover the reverse side of the hand with patterned paper.

5 Glue the support shape to the patterned paper and cut around the shape with a craft knife, trimming off the excess paper as before.

1 Trace the templates on page 120 for the hand shape and the support, and transfer to the foam board (see page 11).

2 Cut out the foam-board hand and support shapes using a craft knife.

3 Using a glue stick or spray glue, stick the hand shape onto a piece of patterned paper and cut around the shape with a craft knife.

6 Using quick-drying glue, stick the support to the back of the hand. It needs to be centered and flush with the base of the hand.

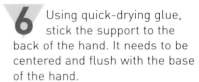

tools and materials

Glue stick

2 pieces patterned paper, about 7 in. x 4 in.
    per decoration

Templates on page 121

Tracing paper

Masking tape

Pencils (No. 3 and No. 2)

Scissors

Craft knife

Ruler

Cutting mat

Scorer

Hole punch

Fuse wire or wire from freezer bag ties

Pliers

Thread or thin ribbon

These holiday decorations were inspired by the shapes used in the designs of the 1960s and 1970s. Try using a different pattern on each one while keeping to an overall color theme, like this one of blues, greens, and silver. The decorations look very pretty dangling from white-painted twigs, catching the light as they gently twist and turn.

holiday
decorations

1 Using a glue stick, stick the two rectangles of patterned paper together to make a double-sided piece.

2 Trace the three template shapes on page 121 for the decoration and transfer to the paper (see page 11).

3 Cut out the shapes using scissors for the outer edges and a craft knife for the inner sections. Take care not to cut the scoring lines.

4 Score the large piece where indicated on the template.

5 Fold all the flaps on the large piece, bending them backward and forward on alternate rows.

6 Punch small holes in each piece where indicated on the template.

7 Thread the wire through the holes in each section and join into small loops that link the sections together. Snip off any excess wire with the pliers.

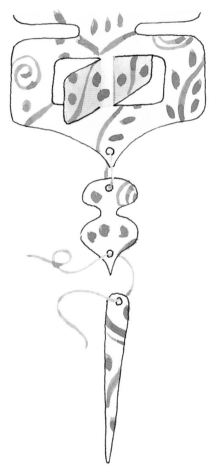

8 Pass a length of thread or a thin piece of ribbon through the hole at the top of the decoration for hanging it up.

flowers and frills **45**

tools and materials

String
Ruler
Scissors
Masking tape
Pencil
1 sheet thin cardstock, 20 in. x 20 in.
Pushpin
Clothes pin
Newspaper
Wallpaper paste or diluted white school glue
Paintbrush
Candies
Tissue paper in several colors, 30 in. x 20 in.
Glue stick

festive
piñata

The tradition of breaking open a decorated clay pot to release the candies and coins within is hundreds of years old. Today, piñatas made from papier-mâché are still used around the world to celebrate special occasions.

Children will love helping to create this papier-mâché piñata. Fill it with candy, hang it by a string, and let each child take turns in hitting it with a cardboard tube until one of them finally breaks the piñata and the candies spill out.

1 Cut a piece of string 10¹/₄ in. long. Using a small piece of masking tape, attach the string to the pencil close to the lead. Find the middle (approximately) of the piece of cardstock. Stick a pushpin through the free end of the string to pin it to the cardstock. Now, with the string taut, swing the pencil around to draw a circle about 20 in. in diameter.

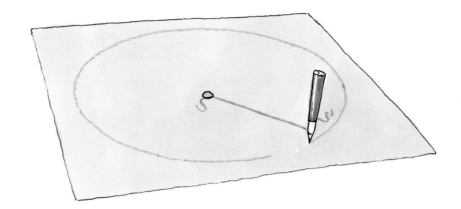

2 Use scissors to cut out the circle. Fold it in half, then cut along the fold line to form two semicircles. Form one half into a cone shape, then overlap the edges and secure with masking tape. Repeat with the other semicircle to make an identical cone, placing it over the first one to achieve the same circumference.

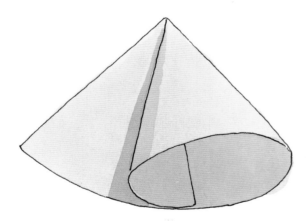

3 To hang the piñata, tie a piece of string securely to a clothes pin or something similar, then push the string out through the top of one of the cones so that the pin remains inside the cone.

4 Using masking tape, attach the bases of the two cones to each other to make a single shape.

5 Make the papier-mâché. Tear up strips of
newspaper into pieces roughly 3 1/2 in. x 3 in.
in size. Brush the pieces of newspaper with
wallpaper paste and attach them to the cardstock
shape, covering it all over. Remember that you will
only need to apply a layer or two of newspaper to
the piñata—if you make it too thick it will be
impossible to break!

7 You may find it helpful to rest the piñata in
a vase while you are decorating it. Cut strips
of tissue paper measuring about 30 in. x 2 1/2 in.
Cut a fringe along the length of each strip, leaving
a 3/4-in. gluing strip. Using a glue stick, glue the
fringe border around the piñata. Glue on the rest
of the fringes in layers, so that each fringe overlaps
the glue strip of the fringe below it.

6 Wait for the papier-mâché to dry
(usually overnight if two layers
have been applied). Cut a small
opening and insert the candies into
the piñata. Use masking tape to
reseal the opening.

printed matter

tools and materials

Scrap paper, such as old school notebooks
Scissors
Craft knife
Ruler
Cutting mat
2 sheets thicker paper or thin cardstock, $5^1/_2$ in. x $5^1/_2$ in.
Template on page 120
Tracing paper
Masking tape
Pencils (No. 3 and No. 2)
Bulldog clips
Hammer hole punch or bradawl
Hammer
Toothpicks
Darning needle
Thin string/strong thread/waxed cotton, 32 in.
Scraps for cover decoration, such as labels
Glue stick

This little notebook is made using Japanese bookbinding methods. Once you have worked your way through the instructions, you will realize how easy it is. You may be inspired to use this method to create sketchbooks, journals, and scrapbooks. Personalize your books by covering them with scraps, photos, or attractive origami papers.

japanese bound
notebook

1 Make the pages for the notebook: cut out pieces of paper measuring 5½ in. x 5½ in. Make as many as you need to create a notebook of the thickness you desire. A good source is unused pages cut from school notebooks that were brought home at the end of the year.

2 Make the cover. Cut out two pieces of thick paper or thin cardstock the same size as the pages. The covers of school notebooks are good for this, if there is a clean area that is large enough.

3 Trace the template on page 120 and transfer the positions of the five holes to one of the covers (see page 11).

4 Place the pages between the two covers. Use bulldog clips to clamp everything together. Use a bradawl or a hammer hole punch and a hammer to make the holes through the pages. Place a toothpick in each hole as you complete it, to keep the pages in line.

5 Now bind the book. Thread the darning needle with 32 in. of string, strong thread, or waxed cotton. Starting at the third hole, lift up a few pages and thread the string through the hole to come out through the cover. Pull the string through, leaving 1 in. of string lying along the spine in between the pages.

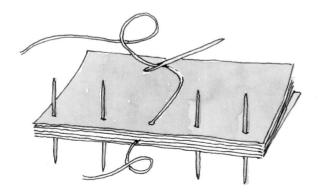

6 Take the needle down through the fourth hole, around the spine, then down through the fourth hole again.

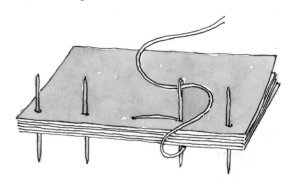

7 Bring the needle up through the fifth hole, then take it around the spine and up through the fifth hole again.

8 Take the needle around the edge of the book and bring it up through the fifth hole again. Move back to the fourth hole and take the needle down through it.

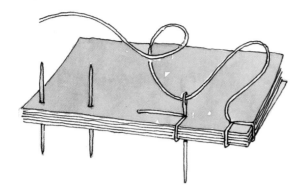

9 Bring the needle up through the second hole, then take it over the spine and up through the second hole again.

10 Move along to the first hole and take the needle down through it. Bring the needle around the spine then down through the first hole again.

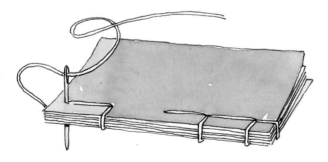

11 Take the needle around the edge of the book and then down through the first hole.

12 Bring the needle up through the second hole, then move along to the third hole and take the needle down through it.

13 Take the needle around the spine and down through the third hole.

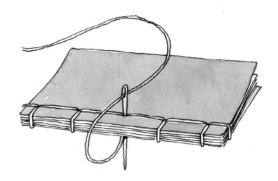

14 Slip the needle under the threads, then pull it through the loop to form a tight knot.

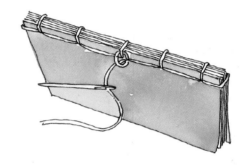

15 Push the needle back up through the third hole and cut the leftover thread flush with the front of the book.

16 You can decorate the book in any way you desire, perhaps gluing on old labels to complete the recycled look.

framed cutouts

skill level

tools and materials

Photocopier or graph paper
Templates on page 120
Tracing paper
Masking tape
Pencils (No. 3 and No. 2)
Tissue paper in three
    contrasting colors

Scissors
Craft knife
Ruler
Cutting mat
White paper or thin cardstock,
    8 in. x 10 in.
Spray glue
Clip frame, 8 in. x 10 in.

This project is a great opportunity to experiment with color. Cut out shapes in different shades and play around with them. Turn them this way and that, overlay and reverse them until you come up with a layout you are happy with. Whether you hang a single picture on the wall or group several pictures together, you'll create a stylish and contemporary focal point in your home.

1 Use a photocopier or the graph-paper method (see page 10) to enlarge the templates on page 120 by 200 percent, onto a tabloid size sheet of paper. Trace the templates and transfer them to the tissue paper (see page 11). Cut out a variety of shapes from the three colors of tissue paper. Before discarding scraps, check for shapes to add to your design.

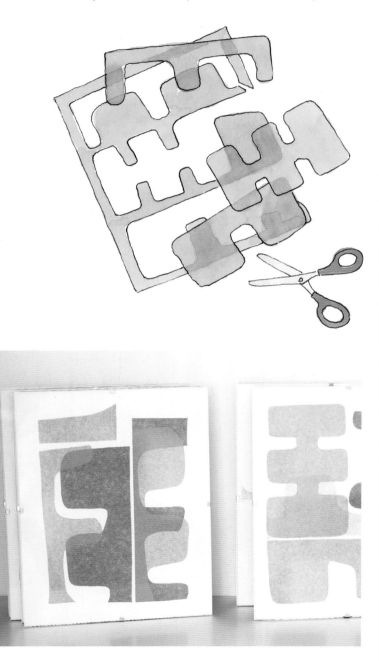

2 Start laying down different combinations of colors and shapes of tissue paper on the cardstock.

3 When you are happy with the layout, glue the pieces in position using spray glue.

4 Place the artwork inside the clip frame to complete the project.

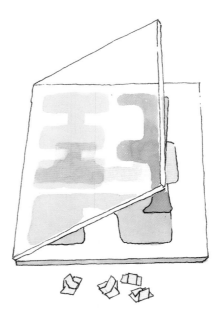

tools and materials
Spray glue
Patterned paper, 8 in. x 12 in. per icosahedron
Thin cardstock, 8 in. x 12 in. per icosahedron
Photocopier or graph paper
Template on page 123
Tracing paper
Masking tape
Pencil (No. 3)
Pin
Ruler
Craft knife
Cutting mat
Scorer
Strong, quick-drying glue

These geometric shapes look great in contrasting colors and patterns. Have fun displaying them in different combinations to create an ever-changing sculpture that you can display on a sideboard or shelf or use as an impressive centerpiece for the dinner table. It's sure to be a talking point!

stacking
icosahedrons

1 Use spray glue to stick the patterned paper to the cardstock (or use patterned cardstock).

2 Use a photocopier or the graph-paper method (see page 10) to enlarge the template on page 123 by 200 percent, onto a tabloid size sheet of paper. Trace the template, then place the tracing paper on the cardstock, secure with masking tape and use a pin to prick through the corner points. Remove the tracing paper and join the points using a pencil and ruler.

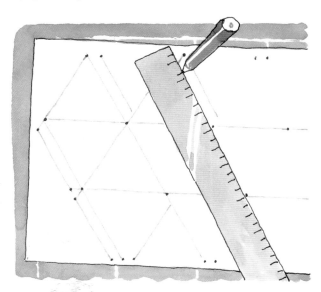

4 Fold the scored lines, one by one, to form the 3-D shape. Apply quick-drying glue to each flap and secure in position. Repeat the steps to make further icosahedrons.

3 Cut out the shape. Score along all the lines, including the gluing flaps.

skill level

tools and materials
Pages from an unwanted book
Pencils (No. 3 and No. 2)
Ruler
Scissors
Glue stick
Template on page 119
Tracing paper
Masking tape
Ribbon or string

paper flowers

These flowers have been made from the leaves of an old book. Here they have been fashioned into a garland, but they have many decorative uses. You could use them to top a wrapped-up present or secure one to a piece of chunky, homemade soap. Stick one to a wooden clothes pin to create an attractive clip for keeping letters and papers together.

1 Make the inner part of the flower. Cut out a strip of paper measuring 2¹/₄ in. x 13³/₄ in. Cut into a fringe along the whole length, snipping three-quarters of the way across the width. It doesn't matter if the cuts are not exactly the same distance apart.

2 Spread glue along the uncut edge, avoiding the fringing, then roll up the strip tightly.

3 Trace the template for the petal on page 119 and transfer it to the paper (see page 11). Cut out four petals. Fix each petal to the fringed center by gluing the base of the petal to the rolled-up strip.

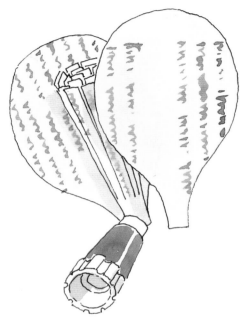

4 When all the petals are in position, bend the base of the flower into a U-shape and allow to dry. The U-shape makes it easier to attach the flower and you can tie or glue on a piece of ribbon or string here.

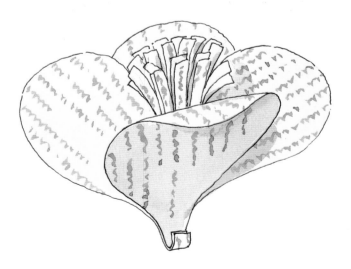

tools and materials

Computer or stencil
Photocopier or graph paper
Tracing paper
Masking tape
Pencils (No. 3 and No. 2)
Thin cardstock
Craft knife
Ruler
Cutting mat
Scissors
Glue stick
Scraps for decoration, such as old music scores,
    stamps, candy papers, wrapping paper

3-D letters

These 3-D letters make great decorations for a child's bedroom. They are also perfect as gifts, as you can personalize them for the recipient and create something unique each time by sticking on all sorts of different decoration.

1 Print out your chosen letter from a computer as large as possible or draw it using a stencil. Using a photocopier, keep enlarging the letter until it reaches the desired size. Alternatively, scale it up with the graph-paper method (see page 10).

2 Trace the letter and transfer it to the cardstock (see page 11). Cut out two letter shapes to make the top and bottom pieces. If your letter will be seen only from the front (for example, if you plan to place it on a mantelpiece), cut out just one letter shape.

3 Cut strips of cardstock to make the edging for the sides of the letter. It's a good idea to make these the width of your ruler (often about 1^1/$_2$ in.) so that you don't have to keep measuring and drawing out the lines.

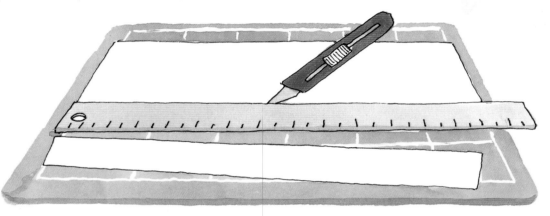

4 Place the edging around the letter shape, holding it at a right angle, and secure it with masking tape. On long edges, using short strips of tape positioned at a right angle to the base may be easiest. When placing edging around a curve, you'll need to cut the tape so that it fans out.

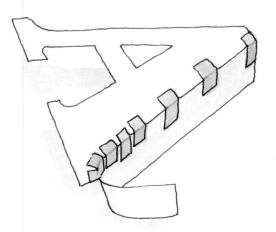

5 When you reach a corner, crease the strip of cardstock and continue to move around the shape. You may find it easiest to work with small lengths of edging, joining the next strip with a piece of masking tape.

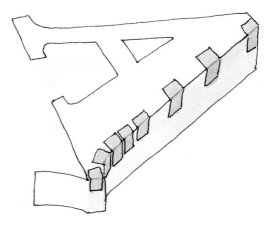

6 Attach the second letter shape to the edging strip as above (omit this step if your letter will have only one side).

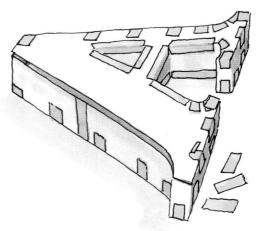

7 Now comes the fun part! Decorate the letter by gluing on candy wrappers, scraps from magazines, wrapping paper, old labels, or stamps. The masking tape will be covered by the decoration.

skill level

✂

tools and materials

Photocopier or graph paper
Templates on page 121
Tracing paper
Masking tape
Pencils (No. 3 and No. 2)
Craft knife
Foam board, 8 in. x 16¹/₂ in. x ¹/₄ in.
   per small airplane

Foam board, 13¹/₂ in. x 26³/₄ in. x ¹/₄ in.
   per large airplane
Ruler
Cutting mat
Old maps, to cover foam board
Spray glue
Hole punch
String
Clear tape

airplane **mobile**

So simple to make, these airplanes are an original decoration for a child's bedroom. Hang them over the bed and encourage dreams of travel to faraway places. For the decoration, you can use sections from an old road atlas or old maps you've discovered in secondhand stores.

1 To make the small plane, use a photocopier or the graph-paper method (see page 10) to enlarge the templates on page 121 by 200 percent, onto a tabloid size sheet of paper. Trace the templates and transfer them to the foam board (see page 11).

2 Cut out a body, wingpiece, and tailpiece from the foam board. Cut out the slots.

3 Position the foam-board shapes on the pieces of map and attach them using spray glue. Use a craft knife to cut out each map-covered shape. Turn over the shapes, position them on a new piece of map and repeat to cover the other side.

4 Trim off any excess paper around the edges. Recut all the slots now covered by map paper.

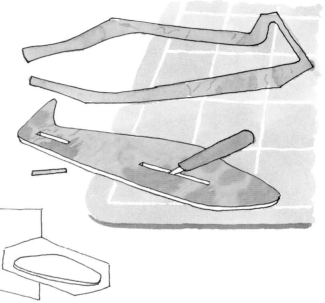

5 Push the wingpiece and tailpiece through the slots on the body.

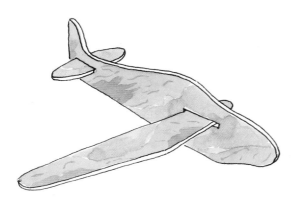

6 Using a hole punch, make two small holes as shown in the illustration. Thread each with a piece of string to hang the airplane.

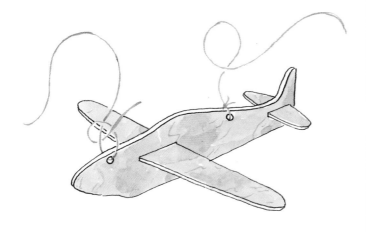

7 To make the large plane, you need to enlarge the templates in sections. Use the 200 percent enlargement you made for the small plane. First, enlarge the tailpiece by 150 percent on a letter size sheet of paper. Then enlarge the body and wing by 150 percent in two sections, onto tabloid size sheets of paper. Use clear tape to attach these at the join line (marked on the template). The slots will have increased in width during the enlarging process and need to be redrawn to a width of 1/4 in. to match the thickness of the foam board. The templates for the large plane are now ready to use.

skill level

tools and materials

Photocopier or graph paper
Template on page 125
Clear tape
Tracing paper
Masking tape
Pencil
Thin white cardstock:
12 in. x 16$\frac{1}{2}$ in. for small cube
13 in. x 17$\frac{3}{4}$ in. for medium cube
15$\frac{3}{4}$ in. x 21$\frac{1}{4}$ in. for large cube
Pin
Ruler
Craft knife
Cutting mat
Scorer
Strong, quick-drying glue
Black-and-white photographs
Black-and-white patterned paper:
4 in. x 4 in. per side to be covered of
     small cube
4$\frac{1}{2}$ in. x 4$\frac{1}{2}$ in. per side to be covered
     of medium cube
5 in. x 5 in. per side to be covered of
     large cube
Glue stick or white school glue

These photo cubes have a really contemporary look. Place photos on three or four side panels of each cube and fill the remaining panels with black-and-white patterned paper in various designs. Strong, graphic designs will complement the black-and-white photographs.

monochrome
photo cubes

1 To make the small cube, use a photocopier or the graph-paper method (see page 10) to enlarge the template on page 125 by 200 percent, onto two tabloid size sheets of paper. Use clear tape to attach the two sheets at the join line, then trace the template and transfer it to the cardstock. The easiest way of doing this is to place the tracing paper on the cardstock and use a pin to prick through all the corner points. Remove the tracing paper and join the points using a pencil and ruler.

2 Cut out the shapes. Score along all the gluing flaps and other scoring lines.

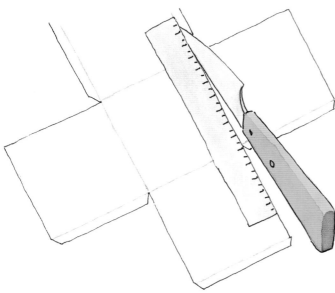

3 Bend along the scoring lines. Assemble the cubes by gluing the flaps in position with quick-drying glue.

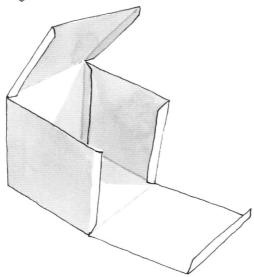

4 Cut out photographs and patterned paper to fit the panels of the cubes.

5 Glue the decorations in place using a glue stick or white school glue.

6 To make different sizes of cube, it is easiest to redraw the template straight onto the thin cardstock you are using for the cube. For a medium cube, each face should measure 4 1/2 in. x 4 1/2 in. For a large cube, each face should measure 5 in. x 5 in. The gluing flaps on all the cubes are 1/2 in. wide.

skill level

tools and materials

Photocopier or graph paper
Templates on page 124
Tracing paper
Masking tape
Pencils (No. 3 and No. 2)
Thin white cardstock, 2 pieces: 13$3/4$ in. x 9 in.
Corrugated cardboard, 2 pieces: 12 in. x 16$1/2$ in.
Craft knife
Ruler
Cutting mat
Hammer hole punch with three interchangeable
    heads, $1/16$ in., $1/8$ in., and $3/16$ in. in diameter
Hammer
Strong, quick-drying glue

A few simple cuts and scores transform a piece of white cardstock into a charming panel featuring a pigeon motif. This decorative panel provides a lovely textural contrast with the functional brown corrugated cardboard used for the rest of the letter rack.

corrugated cardboard
letter rack

1 Use a photocopier or the graph-paper method (see page 10) to enlarge the templates on page 124 by 200 percent onto tabloid size paper. Trace the templates and transfer to the corrugated cardboard or white cardstock (see page 11). Note that the white cardstock back panel and corrugated front panel templates are shown on top of the corrugated backing template. When tracing the pigeon motif, carefully mark lines for cutting and lines for scoring.

2 Cut out all the pieces, then cut out and score all the lines for the pigeon motif. For this project, use a craft knife (with a slightly used blade) for scoring, applying it very gently so it just breaks the surface of the cardstock. Bend forward all the sections that have been scored.

3 Punch holes where indicated on the motif. For accurate positioning, it is easiest to use a hammer hole punch with at least three different sizes of head.

4 Now make the white cardstock box section that will hold the letters. Score along the side and front gluing flaps, then bend into shape.

5 Glue the white box section to the white back panel using strong, quick-drying glue.

6 Glue the corrugated front panel to the front of the white box section.

7 Glue the white back panel plus completed box section to the corrugated cardboard backing.

stylish
statements

tools and materials
1 large sheet patterned paper, 12 in. x 16½ in. per carton
1 large sheet thin cardstock, 12 in. x 16½ in. per carton
Spray glue
Photocopier or graph paper
Template on page 122
Clear tape
Tracing paper
Masking tape
Pencils (No. 3 and No. 2)
Craft knife
Ruler
Cutting mat
Scorer
Hole punch
Thin wire, 3 in. per carton
Long-nosed pliers

These little cartons are simple to construct and make lovely gift boxes or party bags (you could even make mini cartons to decorate the Christmas tree). If you prefer, you can use thin patterned cardstock instead of wrapping paper stuck to cardstock.

cardstock and wire
cartons

5 Fold the cardstock along the scoring line at the corner section in between the two holes. This forms a triangle. Bend the triangle to the side so that it lies against the side of the carton.

1 Glue the paper to the cardstock using spray glue.

2 Use a photocopier or the graph-paper method (see page 10) to enlarge the template on page 122 by 200 percent. If you are photocopying, you will need to enlarge the template in two sections, onto tabloid size sheets of paper. Use clear tape to attach these at the join line (marked on the template). Using tracing paper, transfer the template to the cardstock (see page 11). Cut out the shape.

3 Mark the scoring lines and places where the holes are to be punched. Score along all the lines and punch out the holes.

4 Gently crease the scoring lines around the square base.

6 Move along to the next corner section and repeat. Fold in toward the previous corner section so that the four holes are now overlapping.

7 Repeat Steps 5 and 6 on the other side of the carton, so that the four holes are overlapping.

8 Push the wire through the lined-up holes on one side of the carton, then use pliers to bend back about $1/2$ in. of wire inside the carton to secure.

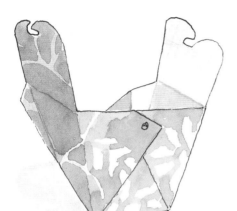

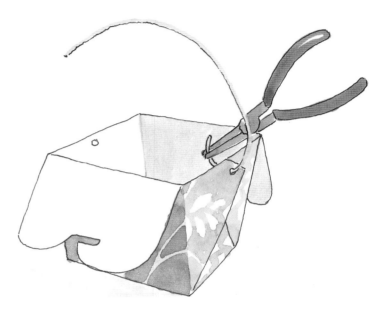

9 Curve the wire over the top of the carton and push the other end through the other holes, bending it back to secure.

10 Hook the two lid flaps together to complete the carton.

tools and materials

Templates on page 123
Tracing paper
Masking tape
Pencils (No. 3 and No. 2)
Thin, pretty paper (we used 20 in. x 30 in. of gift wrap)
Scissors
Craft knife
Ruler
Cutting mat
Chest of drawers
Spray glue or white school glue
Mat varnish
Glass handles (optional)

Originating in Venice 300 years ago, découpage is the art of applying cutouts to a surface and then varnishing. It is a lovely way to turn a plain dresser into something very special. This one is finished with glass handles to complete the vintage look. You can play around with the template layout to customize any item of furniture.

découpage chest of drawers

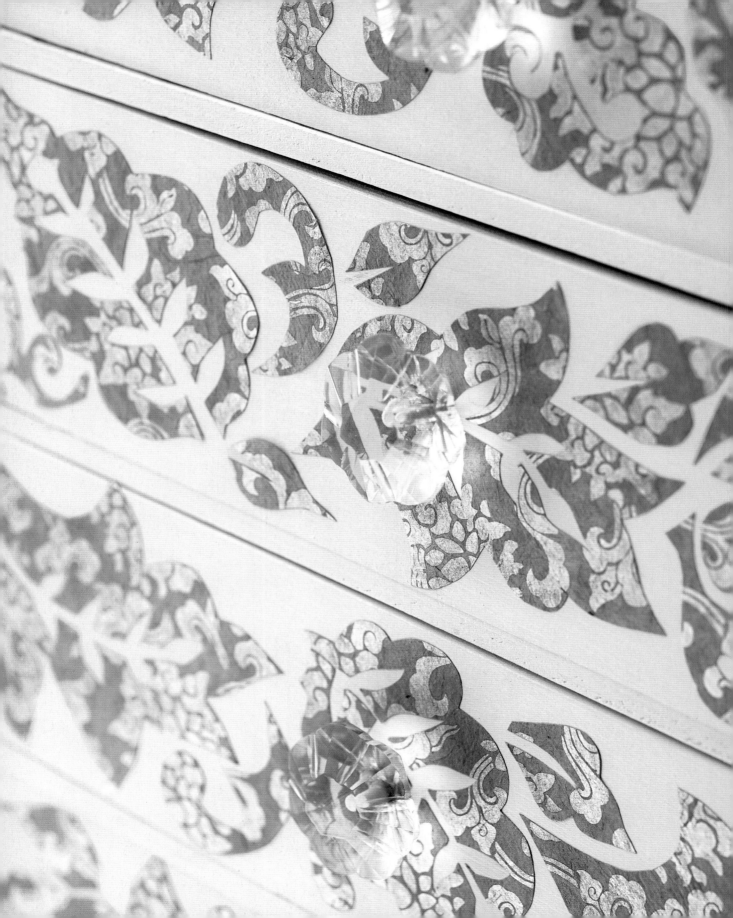

1 Trace the templates on page 123 and transfer the shapes to the thin paper (see page 11). For variation, turn the tracing paper over to create reverse shapes. Cut them out.

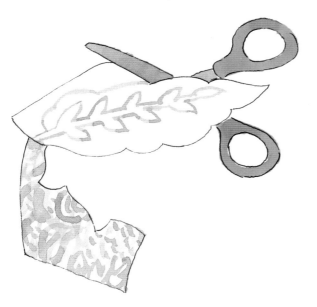

2 Place the shapes on the area you want to cover and move them around until you are happy with the design.

3 Glue the shapes with spray or white school glue and allow to dry.

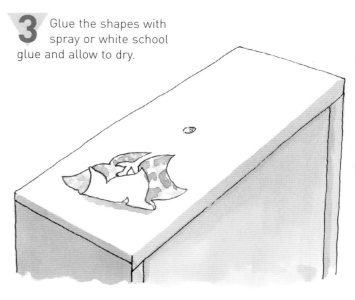

4 Give the chest of drawers a couple of coats of mat varnish. When it is dry, screw on the glass handles if using.

tools and materials
Bowl for mold
Plastic wrap
Newspaper
Papier-mâché paste
Paintbrush
White paint (optional)
Templates on page 118
Tracing paper
Masking tape
Pencils (No. 3 and No. 2)
Thin blue paper
Craft knife
Ruler
Cutting mat

Papier-mâché originated in China, where paper itself was invented. From there, the technique eventually spread to Europe. The term *papier-mâché* is French and means "chewed paper." This little bowl is covered with triangles of blue paper, which create an interesting effect.

papier-mâché bowl

1 Find an existing bowl to use as a mold. Invert it, cover the outside with plastic wrap and set it on a table.

2 Tear off small pieces of newspaper to make the papier-mâché. Brush each piece with papier-mâché paste and apply to the mold until it is completely covered. Repeat with two further layers of newspaper.

3 Allow to dry overnight. Trim off any rough edges and remove the papier-mâché bowl from the mold. If your blue paper is very thin, apply a coat of white paint to cover the newsprint and allow to dry before attaching the paper triangles.

4 Trace the triangle templates on page 118 and transfer to the blue paper (see page 11). Cut out lots of elongated triangles, and fewer of the smaller triangles (these will go around the rim).

5 Starting on the outside of the bowl, in the middle of the base, begin sticking on the triangles with wallpaper paste. Place the thin part of the triangle at the center of the bowl. Continue around the bowl, fanning out the triangles as you go. You will find it helpful to place the bowl over a glass or something similar while you work on it.

6 When you reach the rim of the bowl, fold the triangles over into the inner part of the bowl.

7 When you have completed the exterior of the bowl, allow it to dry. You can place it over the mold to help it keep its shape while drying.

8 Cover the inside of the bowl, starting at the base and overlapping the triangles in rows as you work upward.

9 To finish off the rim neatly, stick smaller triangles all around it.

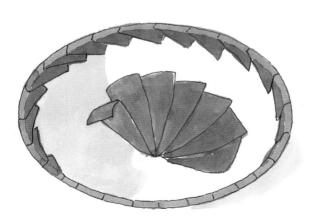

skill level

tools and materials

Photocopier or graph paper
Templates on pages 123
Tracing paper
Masking tape
Patterned thin cardstock or thick paper,
   8 in. x 12 in. per icosahedron
Patterned thin cardstock or thick paper,
   6$\frac{1}{4}$ in. x 7 in. per star point
Pencil
Pin
Ruler
Craft knife
Cutting mat
Scorer
Strong, quick-drying glue

The icosahedron, a geometric shape with 20
triangular faces, is used as the base of this large
star. Made with thin cardstock or thick paper,
the star is sturdy enough to sit on a shelf or
mantelpiece and makes a stunning decoration
for the holidays or any festive occasion.

sculptural star

1 Use a photocopier or the graph-paper method (see page 10) to enlarge the icosahedron template on page 123 by 200 percent, onto tabloid size paper. Transfer to tracing paper, then lay the tracing paper on the patterned cardstock, secure with masking tape and prick through the corner points with a pin. Join up the points using a ruler and pencil.

2 Cut out the shape. Score along all the lines, remembering to score the gluing flaps.

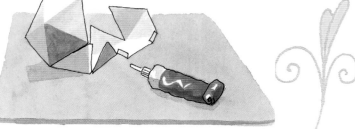

3 Fold the scored lines, one by one, to form the 3-D shape. Apply the glue to each flap and secure in position. This creates the icosahedron shape, which provides the base for the star.

4 Use a photocopier or the graph-paper method (see page 10) to enlarge the star point template on page 123 by 200 percent. Use tracing paper to reproduce this on patterned cardstock as you did in Step 1. You will need to make 20 star points.

5 Cut out the star point shapes, score along the lines and then fold each shape to form a tall pyramid.

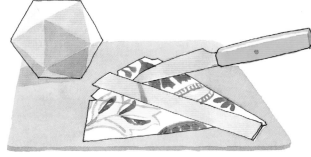

6 Take a star point shape and glue the long flap in place.

7 Fold in the glue flaps at the base of the star point and glue onto one face of the icosahedron. Place in a tall glass or vase for safekeeping while preparing the next star point.

8 Repeat the process with the remaining shapes, building up one star point at a time until the star is complete.

ornate
picture frame

tools and materials

Old picture frame (optional)

Thick white cardstock, 10 in. x 10 in. or to fit
    existing picture frame

Craft knife

Cutting mat

Scissors

Strong, quick-drying glue

Templates on page 121

Tracing paper

Masking tape

Pencils (No. 3 and No. 2)

Thick white paper, such as cartridge paper

This project will give you the satisfaction of creating something elegant out of a simple piece of white paper. You'll find that forming the scrolls from the scored paper takes practice but, once you get the hang of it, you will discover that the process goes quickly and is lots of fun.

1 For a flat frame, cut a hollow rectangle of thick cardstock measuring 8 in. x 8 in. with a 2$\frac{1}{4}$-in. border. Alternatively, cut the cardstock to fit an existing picture frame, allowing for a 2$\frac{1}{4}$-in. border. Fix the cardstock to the frame with strong, quick-drying glue.

2 Trace the templates on page 121 and transfer to the white paper (see page 11). Scoring lines are marked on the templates, but you can omit these from the tracing if you wish as variation in the scoring will add to the design. You will produce 27 pieces in total, made from two scroll shapes and two leaf shapes. Some are reversed: turn the tracing over to transfer these. Cut out all the shapes.

3 In this project, you need to score with a craft knife (with a slightly used blade), applying a gentle pressure to just cut the surface of the paper without going right through it. Place the tip of the craft knife at the center of the pointed part of a scroll or leaf and draw it around in a curve to meet the center of the base of the shape.

4 Now comes the tricky bit: gently squeeze a scroll into a 3-D shape along the scoring line (or lines). Push the rounded end gently in a spiral movement and it will, with a bit of practice, go into the right shape. Once you get the hang of the first one, the others will follow easily.

5 Creating the leaves is easy: just fold gently along the scoring lines.

6 Arrange all the pieces on the base frame and you can then begin to stick them on. Use one blob of glue at the end of each shape. The ends will always be concealed by the next shape that is added.

skill level

tools and materials

Recycled thin cardstock, brown on
   one side and white on the other,
   20 in. x 5 in.
Pencil
Ruler
Craft knife
Cutting mat
Hole punch
Hammer
Brown paper, 6 in. x 2^{1}/$_{2}$ in. (could be
   taken from a paper bag or envelope)

This bowl epitomizes the beauty of cardstock
and paper. Merely by slotting pieces together,
without any glue, you can create something
wonderful. The bowl is not intended to be
used for storing things: cherish it as an
object of beauty, symmetry, and form.

simple bowl

4 Place the five strips of cardstock on top of each other and slot a tube through the hole in each end. They should be a snug fit.

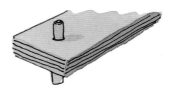

1 Cut five strips of cardstock, each measuring 20 in. x 1 in.

2 Punch an 1/8-in. hole in each end of each strip, positioning it 1/2 in. in from the end and centered. (If your hole punch produces a hole with a bigger diameter, simply increase the size of the strip of paper in the next step so that when it is rolled, it fits tightly into the hole.)

5 Fan out the strips to create a bowl shape. If you want to make the bowl more functional, you could weave strips of cardstock through the middle section, but this will detract from the purity of the design.

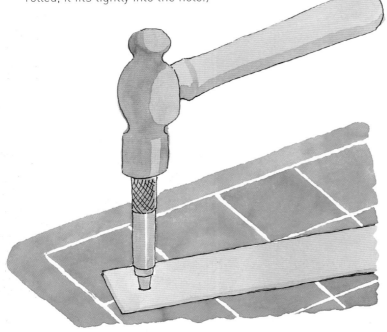

3 Cut two strips of brown paper, 4 in. x 1 1/4 in. Roll these up tightly to create a solid tube.

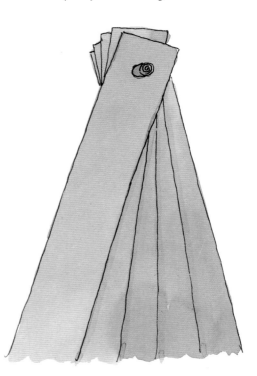

tools and materials

Template on page 126

Tracing paper

Masking tape

Pencils (No. 3 and No. 2)

1 piece thin cardstock, metallic on one side and white on
   the other, 14 in. x 27^1/$_2$ in. per smaller snowflake

2 pieces thin cardstock, metallic on one side and white on
   the other, 21^1/$_2$ in. x 17^3/$_4$ in. per larger snowflake

Scissors

Craft knife

Ruler

Cutting mat

Scorer

Strong, quick-drying glue

Photocopier or graph paper (for larger snowflake)

In wintertime, these metallic
snowflakes make lovely
contemporary decorations.
Hang the snowflakes in the
hall to gently spin as people
walk past or line them up
on a mantelpiece to create a
magical scene.

giant
snowflakes

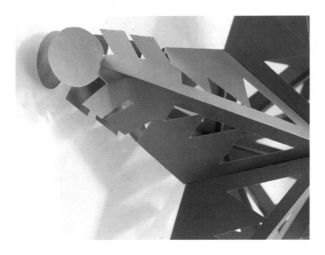

4 Fold in the glue flaps. Fold along the central scoring line, stopping at the end circle. The snowflakes are metallic on one side and white on the other. Fold five pieces with the white facing outward and five pieces with the metallic color facing outward.

5 Take one white piece and one colored piece. Glue together using the two smaller glue flaps. Repeat with the remaining pieces to make a total of five snowflake points.

1 To make the smaller snowflake, trace the template on page 126 and transfer it to the cardstock (see page 11). Mark a dot where the central scoring line finishes. Repeat to make ten outlines.

2 Cut out the 10 pieces. It is easiest to use sharp scissors to do this. Use a craft knife for cutting out the triangular inner shapes.

3 Score along the glue flaps and down the central scoring line. Do not score inside the end circle.

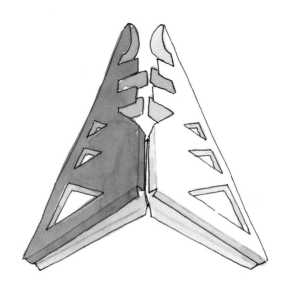

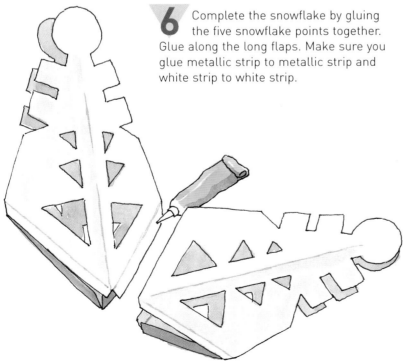

6 Complete the snowflake by gluing the five snowflake points together. Glue along the long flaps. Make sure you glue metallic strip to metallic strip and white strip to white strip.

7 To make the larger giant snowflake, use a photocopier or the graph-paper method (see page 10) to enlarge the template on page 126 by 200 percent, onto a tabloid size sheet of paper. Then continue with the project as for the smaller snowflake.

tools and materials

Photocopier or graph paper
Templates on page 126
Tracing paper
Masking tape
Pencils (No. 3 and No. 2)
Thin white cardstock, 8 in. x 12 in. per shade
Craft knife
Ruler
Cutting mat
Hammer hole punch with three interchangeable
    heads, $1/16$ in., $1/8$ in., and $3/16$ in. in diameter
Hammer
Strong, quick-drying glue or double-sided tape

These shades are inspired by Mexican punched tinware and the method used to make them is similar. You will need a hole punch with three different sizes of head and a hammer. When the shade is placed over a glass with a tealight in it, the light shines through the punched holes and transforms an ordinary sheet of paper into a delicately illuminating piece.

white cardstock
candle shades

1 Use a photocopier or the graph-paper method (see page 10) to enlarge the template and your chosen motif on page 126 by 200 percent. Trace the template and motif, ensuring the motif is positioned centrally as marked. Transfer the template to the cardstock (see page 11), then cut out the shade.

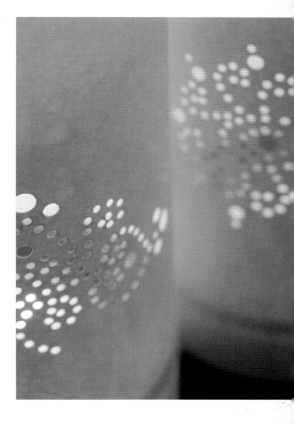

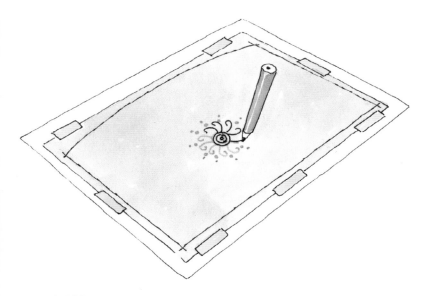

2 Using the hole punch and hammer, start punching holes along the lines of the motif. Punch a series of small holes along the solid lines and use different heads to make the medium and large holes as marked. Make sure you leave a small gap between each hole.

3 Roll the cardstock into a cylinder, fixing the sides together with glue or double-sided tape.

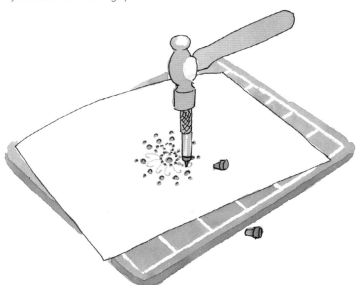

templates

See page 10 for instructions on enlarging templates and page 11 for how to transfer the templates to paper or cardstock using tracing paper.

For downloadable versions of the following templates please go to www.octopusbooks.co.uk/templates.

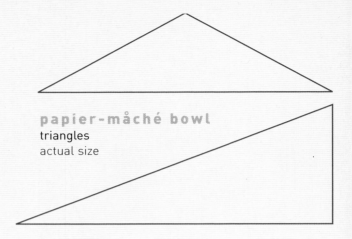

papier-mâché bowl
triangles
actual size

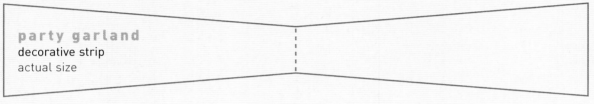

party garland
decorative strip
actual size

KEY
——— cut
- - - - - score / fold

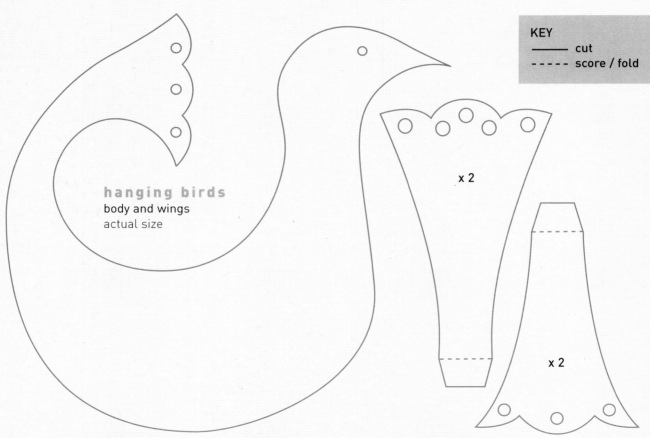

hanging birds
body and wings
actual size

x 2

x 2

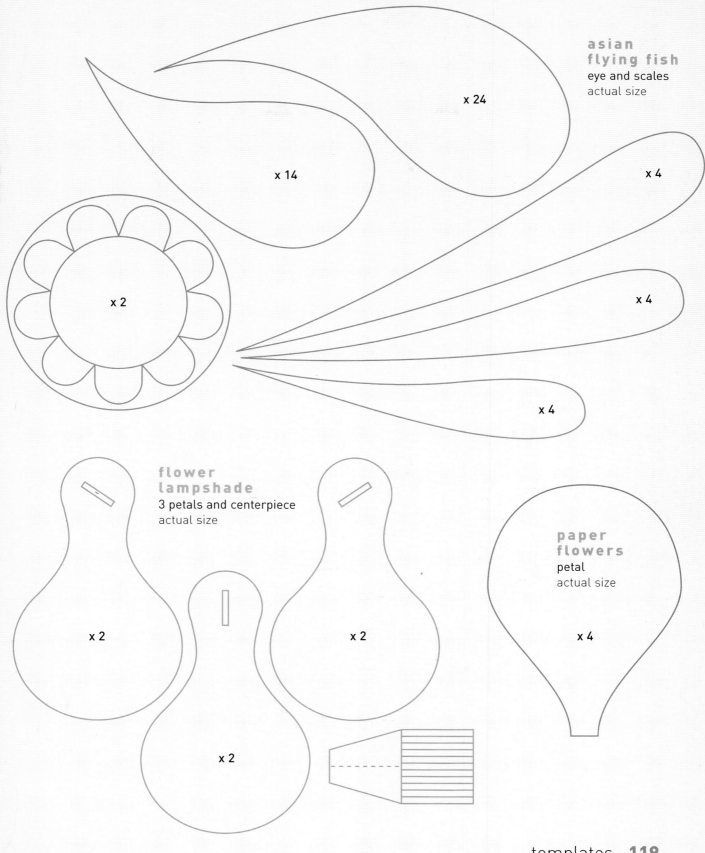

asian flying fish
eye and scales
actual size

x 24

x 14

x 4

x 4

x 4

x 2

flower lampshade
3 petals and centerpiece
actual size

x 2

x 2

x 2

paper flowers
petal
actual size

x 4

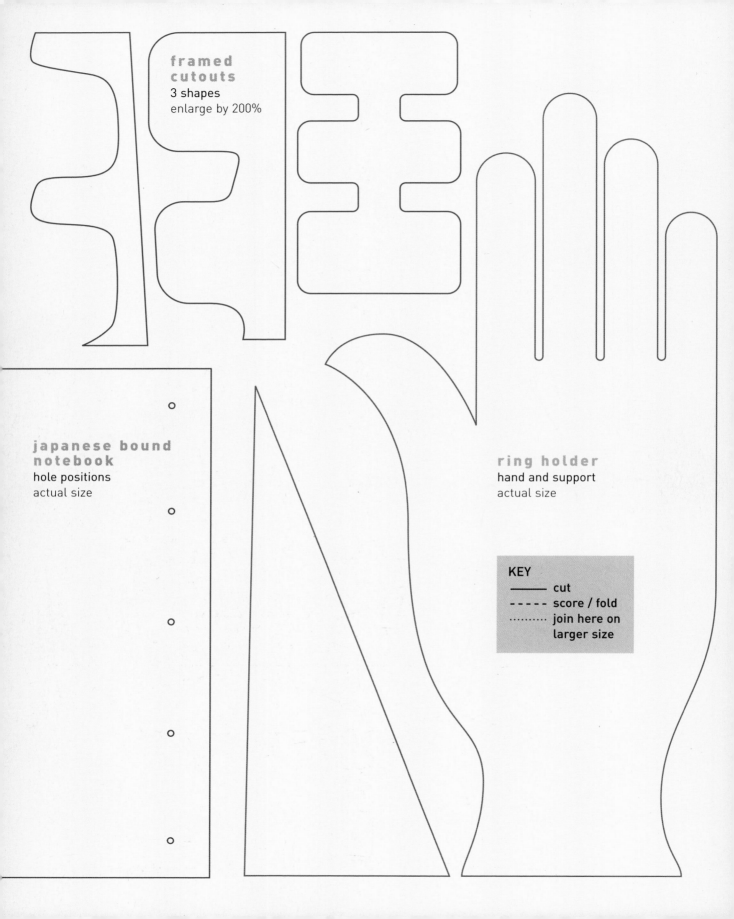

framed
cutouts
3 shapes
enlarge by 200%

japanese bound
notebook
hole positions
actual size

ring holder
hand and support
actual size

KEY
———— cut
- - - - - score / fold
.... join here on
larger size

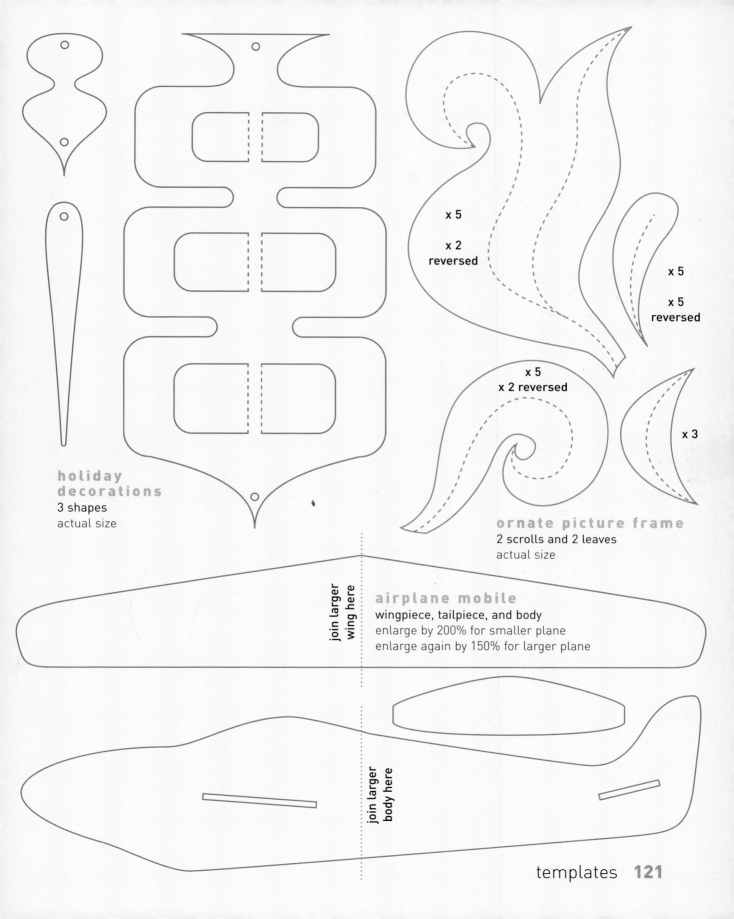

x 5

x 2 reversed

x 5

x 5 reversed

x 5

x 2 reversed

x 3

holiday
decorations
3 shapes
actual size

ornate picture frame
2 scrolls and 2 leaves
actual size

join larger
wing here

airplane mobile
wingpiece, tailpiece, and body
enlarge by 200% for smaller plane
enlarge again by 150% for larger plane

join larger
body here

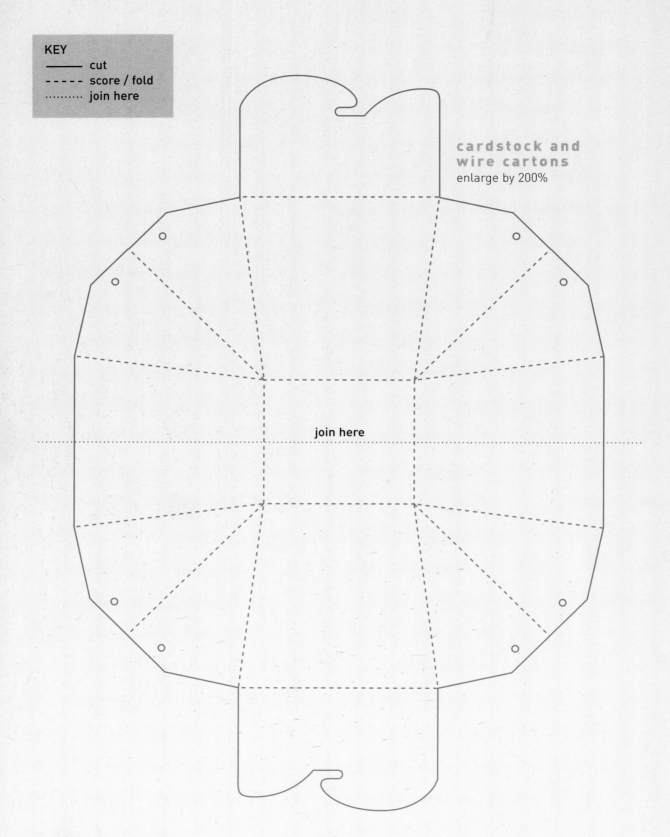

cardstock and
wire cartons
enlarge by 200%

join here

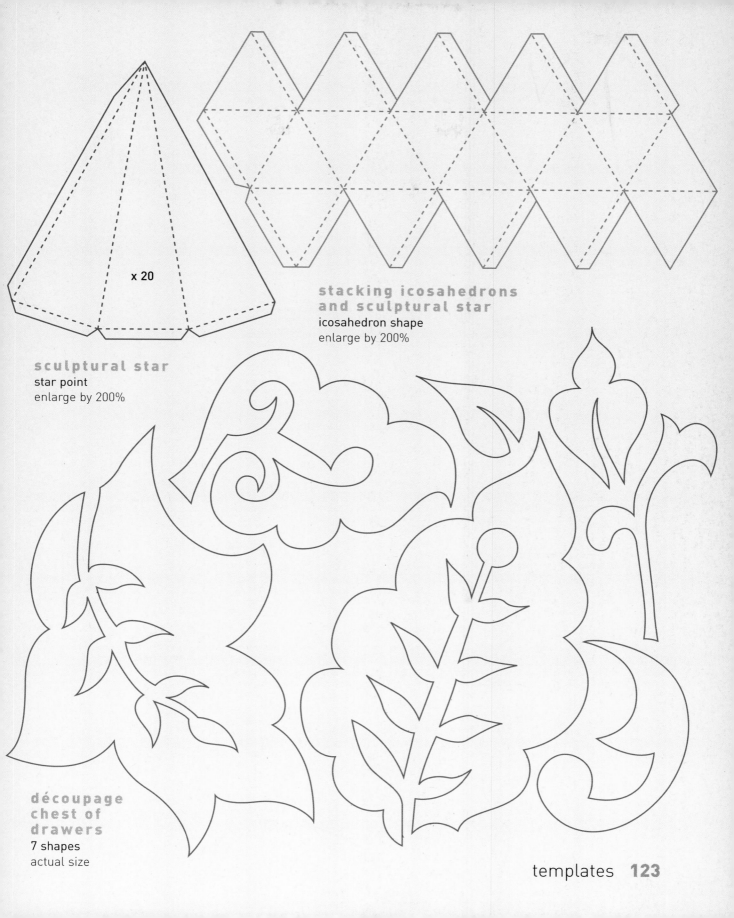

x 20

sculptural star
star point
enlarge by 200%

**stacking icosahedrons
and sculptural star**
icosahedron shape
enlarge by 200%

**découpage
chest of
drawers**
7 shapes
actual size

templates **123**

**corrugated
cardboad
letter rack**
enlarge by 200%

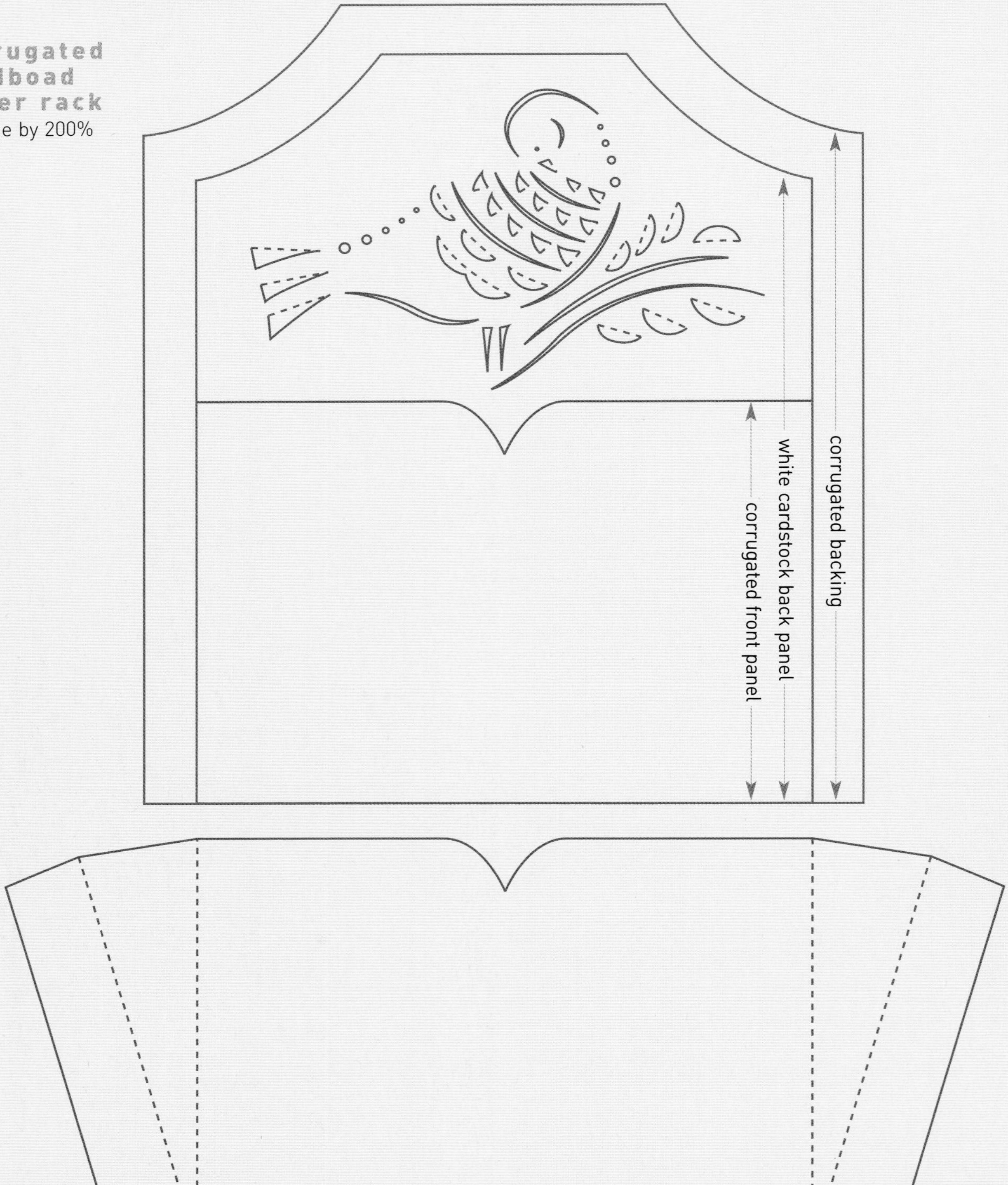

corrugated backing

white cardstock back panel

corrugated front panel

white cardstock box section

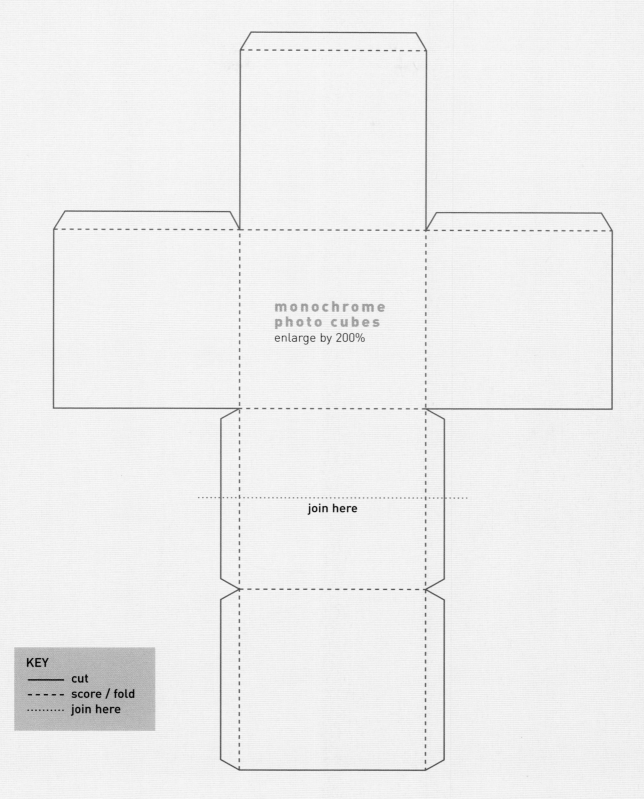

monochrome
photo cubes
enlarge by 200%

join here

KEY
—— cut
----- score / fold
.... join here

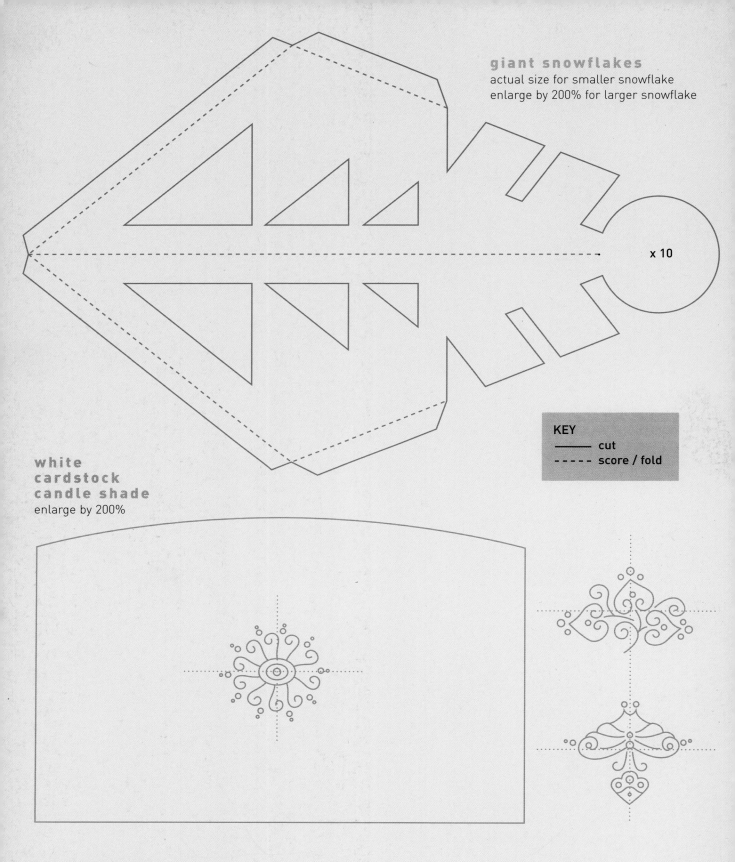

giant snowflakes
actual size for smaller snowflake
enlarge by 200% for larger snowflake

x 10

KEY
——————— cut
- - - - - score / fold

white
cardstock
candle shade
enlarge by 200%

index

acknowledgments

Photography © Octopus Publishing Group
Limited/Sandra Lane

Bird print p.102 www.roddyandginger.co.uk

Executive editor Katy Denny/Jo Lethaby
Senior editor Fiona Robertson
Executive art editor Sally Bond
Designer Janis Utton
Illustrator Kate Simunek/Sudden Impact Media
Production controller Carolin Stransky